SUMMER'S MIXTAPE

AN ECLECTIC & SHORT ANTHOLOGY OF POEMS

MIDSUMMER DREAM HOUSE

Cover Art
Lucy in the Sky
by Dan Ross

Editors
Emma Grey Rose
George du Bois
Melinda Snyder
Jeff Edwards
Andrea Rymer

Midsummer Dream House
San Diego, California
United States

Paperback ISBN: 979-8-9993991-2-0
Printed in the United States

midsummer dream house

CONTENTS

FRAGILE PLACES

A hidden stamp in mirror walls,
I walk afresh dawn up the
ground floor cavern, tucked-away
slots in Morningside Heights
chill.

Shuffle in smart-shoed attire,
cooking speckle-shined for this
crowded exchange, flipping off
a switch in time to save me.

From when that love of brickwork
and high places started to fade
into fantasies of pushing, jumping,
leaping, into the floating fire
escape.

I trap the madness in champagne
expression, glancing pleasantries
tracing the wax of shoelaces,
the falling of triple-redundant
words to marble floor.

A breath outside imagined, cigarettes
and motor oil combining in sweat
sense; makes the moving go by
quicker, picture-perfect marking
time.

DS Maolalai

WHAT REAL LIFE IS MADE OF

this is a hotel room, an open-
room balcony, built
on a hill and hung
down above Dublin
like a frown on a dark
heavy brow. lights under
are neatly laid out
straight as cutlery; tables
with candle-bright
trim. this is the night-
time – and Dublin's
lit up rather beautiful.
it isn't a view of which
real life is made – the stud
which gives shape
to the substance and bone
is not much the thing
in itself. you come
on the balcony,
quiet behind me.
your naked arms bend
on my waist.

"HAJDEMO U PLANINE" BUT I'M THE GIRL

You say not to step upon the sharp rocks but I do,
I do. Triangulate my sole. Balance out of your grip. The
tidal cycle

Keeps my skin immaculate. Tumbled clean
Thin shirt for the hot climate. Off-white.

Repeat: *hot climate*
Trilling tongue, lips catching on the 'm' and watching
you watch me. Me,
too lush to allow by the sea for much longer. Needing to
rip down
veils of Spanish moss for cover.
Da, da, da. Yes, yes, yes.

Foam at our lips and
my dowry in sand dollars,

We dive beneath the trough, emerge having lost our
sunglasses, our eyes

Knotting afterimages into live oak branches, hands
reaching for the breeze captured
in a braid down my spine.

The few passersby (only) take notice of our silhouettes
surfacing.

See you behind
resting your palms on the water like it's a table; you can

"Hajdemo U Planine" but I'm the Girl

slam your fists down and
storm away. In your wake, trailing

I come to shore to find what others have washed up

here;

A beached jellyfish, an averted gaze half-buried. I pass
by, kick the cannonball
back to the surf, flicking no-see-ums off my arms;
now I'm windburnt, stinging–
because summer isn't over and you want to take me
to the mountains to dress in warm clothes. You're
whittling driftwood,
pleading "God, save me,
from the beach," while I–resigned–

strip;

Abandon you to your knife, whitewater dancing
Rings around dead tree limbs,
And let the procession fill my footsteps.

"Hajdemo u Planine" is a song by Yugoslav rock band
Bijelo Dugme. The title translates to "Let's Go to the
Mountains," and it is about a man who wants to leave
the oceanside and go somewhere colder where his girl
will have to wear less revealing clothing.

MY BABY, ODE #8

My baby, she a medley of flavors.
She everything from sweet to umami,
the whole spice shelf and all the herbs, too,
the aromatic temptations of sage
or basil, fresh from garden, supple still
and green, not some dried up crumble, not her.
She the lemony thyme, the tarragon,
the shiso, the spiky sprig of rosemary,
the breath of all the outdoors coming in.
My baby thrills my nose, opens my eyes,
makes my mouth say mm-mm, she so savory.
In bed at night I taste the salt and pepper
rub of her daily exertions on her skin,
her seasoning just for me, her special.
She's red insinuation of paprika,
sweet heat of cinnamon, warmth of cardamom,
zesty bite of ginger, earthy as cumin
and coriander, exotic as saffron.
Mm-mm. I eat my baby up, she so good.

Kenneth Kesner

ALYA

where some live their life in an hour or
no longer than a prayer
that leaves though you don't want to
like when i see her silk lines
those eyes and dreams of sometimes
it must have been a windy afternoon

i'd love to meet again but haven't before
a pilgrimage for those lost within sight
who'll have to stay forever somewhere

Kora Dzbinski

TEXTS FOR WHEN HE ASKS FOR SPACE

i.
do you think black holes
explore each other's
bodies?
do you ever think of
bodies as black
Holes?
piano fingers
digging
darkened mouths
lapping it all
in —

anxious eater //
you make a
meal
of me.

ii.
do you think of our bodies —
in which, I mean,
do you think of
me beyond your
body?

become honeyed fly trap.
become black hole.

dig into stomach. // find
Tissue. // find

Texts for When He Asks for Space

Universe.

and before all this,
a star.

DISMANTLED

They've taken all the frames;
the art, the portraits.
They've taken them all off the walls.
Some left faded rectangles,
like reminders
of doors,
portals to somewhere else.

After they took the frames away
they removed things from shelves.
They took plants.
They took knick-knacks and bric-a-brac.
They took the useful things:
paper
pens
coffee mugs.
The shelves sat empty.
Then they took the shelves.
On walls painted eggshell
the lines that remained
could have been languages
or symbols
or code.

Next went the furniture,
the carpets,
the lamps.
The last item taken away
was the Ficus tree that used to sit
in the corner.

Dismantled

I was never sure if it was artificial
or if it was real.

Somehow, they missed me
here in the dying light,
when they checked the cupboards,
and carried out the trash,
and finally
locked the door behind them.
You'd think it would seem larger now,
here without things to fill the space.

HOUSE OF THE FIFTH DAUGHTER

the baby is crying again so she climbs into the wardrobe
and becomes the queen of frostfruit
beneath her shirt, three crayon-stained hands cling
syrup-sticky
(her siblings think she's a spell)
mama is a perfume ad laughing in the bathtub
the water never boils but something always burns
in the pantry: a bag of lentils two thimbles a dead bee
she makes a feast anyway
they call it royal
she tells them: the stars are watching
if we sleep right they'll fold us into clouds
no rent no hunger no mum screaming at her reflection
nighttime is where she wins
in her room the ceiling peels like bark & reveals a
skyladder
she climbs until the air stops being made of rules
she names herself fifth
not first
never first
first is for girls who get childhood
she got a kingdom

Dorit d'Scarlett

PHASMA

in science she learns the stick insect can become invisible
just by staying very
very still
she practices under the stairs
limbs aligned with broom handles
mouth quiet as splinters
her teacher called them phasmatodea
ghost bugs
the kind no one notices until they move or break

sometimes she holds her breath for so long
she wonders if she's turning into wood
her siblings watch cartoons
dad stares through his phone
mum repaints her lips in the toaster reflection
she keeps still
still
so still

when no one comes looking she grows antennae
listens to the house creak
its wooden bones whisper
we see you
you're not wrong
she doesn't cry anymore just sheds
leaves a paper-thin version of herself under the couch

Hugh Findlay

TAR

hot asphalt blacktop
   shimmering rainbow oil slick
     dancing squirrel feet

Karen Pierce Gonzalez

ONCE A BODY OF WATER

My seafoam hair still soaks up sunlight;
warmth undulates down my spine.
Between my toes, spider crabs, barbed dragon fish,
and eelpouts rest, and, tunneling to land,
my arms form canals –
rainfall and sand pour into my mouth,
open until completely full.

I have become porous and now leak –
droplets of who I am settles into sea beds.

Less fluid, I seek what I have lost.

When I scour the clouds for clues
Raven squawks. *Do not look there.*
Your history is in the sediment below.

Stirred, stories of what may have been forgotten
bubble up from that dark.

EVERYTHING OR NOTHING

                    is stopping me from remembering
you like this. Relaxed shoulders and wet hair, I want
to run my fingers through time. Steal a pear from
the bowl on your kitchen counter. I like seckel pears
sometimes and the way you say my name. Sixteen days
into summer, I feel the heat (read: your fingers) on the
nape of my neck. The mint has really overtaken my
garden, so we're adding it to everything. The pitcher of
lemonade, the chopped salad with feta, and especially
the poems. I don't want to put you in them, but you
settle in beside the mint and hang your denim jacket on
the coat rack by my door.

Zach Spruce

VERNA'S BLOOM

All across the forest floor,
construction-yellow blossoms
burst from dark green hearts
like little nuclear explosions.
It's called lesser celandine,
you believe, *ficaria verna.*
This blanket of poison tendrils
enfolds abandoned sedan's
rusted frame.
The sunny meadow marred
by an ominous shadow—
       Verizon cellular tower
       looms like a cursed spire
where woods marry gravel pits.
It is not enough to pray, to run
your hands across a beech tree,
to read faded love letters scrawled
on guestbooks of silvery bark.
All day you've read Michio Kaiku's
predictions of future humans building
hi-tech / volcanic / lunar caverns.
Meanwhile, half-decayed birds
in whirlpooling sewage, ancient
tortoises slickened with petroleum.
       Sere grass sways with
              the wind like wraiths.
Who's to say, really? Now you meet
the gaze of a Starbuck's maid staring
from littered Styrofoam. Now you think
      what a silly metaphor:
          we are ficaria verna.

AS SPARKS DEPARTING FLAME

You hike the familiar hills
where smoldering cedar
feeds night air, where
deep mud fills mossy trails.
Remember a fireflash—
      cardinals flitting in branches
as sparks departing flame.
Remember fallen oak leaves,
plum lipstick, the hypnosis
of a choir of spring peepers.
Remember your good friend
stoned out of his mind
staring down the concrete
   spillway.
Look at the water—
everchanging, always in motion.
Remember sitting cross-legged
at the edge of the wooden dock
transfixed by moonbeams
undulating
across black mirrors of silent pond.
Remember the sidereal glow
from cigarette cherries, threads
        of smoke unfurling into void
   like veils of withered ivy.

James Broschart

CYCLE, SPIRAL

Trees that held so tightly onto green promise
straight through from tender tips of Spring
stand now stiff and brittle,
while hope escapes their dark fingers
to swirl into malevolent skies.

Birds whose early robust voices
called all forth to attend their joy,
now cry out as each few remaining
pass in search of glean,
already denied from scant harvest.

A stream that once swept mayflies aside
to race with storm clouds and cast rich mud
abroad from within its bounty,
now settles well below its banks
and hunkers down to nurse thin rations.

The coursing Sun, whose rhythms fix
each season's pulse through endless cycle,
now blisters the earth and withers life.
Hanging brazen, a massive cudgel,
it holds hostage all that lie beneath.

Naudia Reeves

LET ME CALL THIS BEAUTIFUL

We share the chore of it:
Rat-rearing. Freshen the litter,
launder the fleece,
chop strawberries into littler strawberries, and
hand them out like Halloween candy.

One night, I get too high and say:
We really are eccentric. I'm just now noticing.

To my left:
Five rats running the playpen's perimeter,
a mischief learning how and where to jump
to satisfy their nature of
"do the one thing they don't want you to do,
then do it again."

I am on our bed, my body a spreading thing,
and in the background, the rustle of ninety toes.

I cannot bring myself to judge it.

Even when unwell, the ceiling off-kilter,
the squeaks and skitters unending.
When a delicate life jumps into your hands
and climbs onto your shoulder
for a better look at the world,
his whiskers a tickle on your cheek,
there is no chore too laborious.

I will vacuum, I will scrub.

Let Me Call This Beautiful

I will fill the bowl with water, with peas.
I will offer the fun of fishing,
of peanut excavation, of ribbon-chasing.
I will take these brief years and
fill them with a love so eccentric, you cannot help but
notice.

MAKING TEA IN LATE OCTOBER

Water suspended on the burner,
misty steam whirling
like youthful ghosts sliding down banisters.
Outside in autumn wind, whispering
elms are freckled with candy-corn orange
and caramel apple red.

Water warms and swirls in cauldron,
flick of a black cat's tail. Cranberry
tea anticipates your return to our porch,
blanketed by tiny pumpkins and mums.

Beginning to boil,
descending sun hastily covered
by cumulonimbus clouds,
faces of children
hidden by sheets.

Popping and bubbling,
croaks of burrowing bullfrogs.
Out the bay window, departed
leaves overwhelm our driveway
where your truck should sit.
Have you found someplace else

to hibernate with someone
who thawed your heart, melting
it into tapered candles
of nutmeg and cloves?

Making Tea in Late October

Should I pour
one cup or two?

THE VANISHING ACT

The definition of insanity, my mother
demanding I watch my little brother, again.

Tromping in the sandbox, he was a rope around my
neck.
Climbing a tree after a squirrel made me a frantic
mother.

Leaping like a monster from the bushes at the postman
he turned me into a screaming bitch.

I, the task master, carried his antics in my pockets
like rocks, the weight heavy as a family secret.

A blunder every time as he darted
like a swallow, the blue of his jacket

there, then gone! The magician's rabbit.
The ship falling off the horizon. A ghost.

The neighborhood his oyster for hours.
Another morning shot, *how could I have lost him?*

I became the raccoon in the dumpster,
rummaging through every vacant lot, back yard, and
hedge.

The sniffer dog at work. My mind obsessed
with a flash of the whites of his tennis shoes.

Until, head down, defeated, I kicked the rocks

The Vanishing Act

off the sidewalk all the way home,

dreading my entry, bereft of an explanation,
my brother, and my big sister badge.

Kirby Michael Wright

SUBURBAN SACRIFICE

Quarter moon yellows
The eastern sky

In the coyote hours
Before sun,

When outlaw dogs
Surround backyard pets.

Howls of hunger
Echo blacktop

On a cold morning
Promising blood.

Teeth flash.
The moon at zenith.

The natural order
Brings rebellion

To our human prison
With tiled roofs.

Michael Theroux

TRANSITIONS

Transitional Awareness
April kisses Winter goodbye

Grey spring rain on Kansas gables
slicking down curved streets
and all my world tilts toward Flagstaff
slipping home slowly to you

Cardinals strut between showers
red wet feathers all ruffled
All the critters bob about happily
seeing the banners of Spring

The old winter weeps softly now
knowing its cold time is past
The trees offer their freshest greens
having waited so patiently, perennial

I have also overwintered
not as tree-patient or as grass soft
but with the promises we made
Perennial promises, winter-proof

Time now to join the cardinal
to open as the new flowers
to the reed-pipe's spring song
Back to home, back to you

PALM FOREST

In the gallery while facing a painting, my head loses a
synapse.
My heart skips a beat.

Leaning against the tree, relieved I catch my breath.
Looking up, a tall thin trunk is standing amid a forest
full of palm trees. West, the sky is graying with a tint of
orange.

It's dusk, meaning soon there will be darkness.

High grasses cover the forest floor. I note,
no visible path out. Go left towards the sunset.
At first step my head swims, knees buckle but weak arms
protect my descent.

Closing eyes—no dusk sky. Laying down—no forest
floor.

Jake Williams

DEGREES OF CAPRICORN

After another storm passes
it could be in any season
great drifts of leaves
a woody sea
evergreen charms,
brightest colours thank fleeting rain
while strewn across damp ground
transmuted skies full moon
one degree of Capricorn
sunshine every now and then
mostly then
moon out of bounds ellipses
every benchmark began in a forest
with no idea of what a benchmark was
along with every box we try to think outside of
night creatures invite us
to join their masquerade
remember the power of not doing
grey dark hills beyond or near
full moon heart bows to Saturn
whatever needs to be written
be written
echoes in every shallow sea
whatever phase of the dreampop moon
bars dissolved in silver light reverb
what does it matter what words may say?
cells of life nourished by Pentland rains
though the great gig in the sky may call
trees talk, maybe a part of us might listen
rain blew in again,

coppery leaves shine
delight shouts to solstice green hills

Amelia Napiorkowski

HIS BELOVED BASKETCASE

It began on a bench,
against a brick building
in an alley of the old town…
Now we're planning our summers in January,
a vasectomy during storytime.
Zoloft sexlessness,
innocently staged seductive scenes…
He's fed up with me.
Go outside, stretch, do *something* - which makes sense
sitting down on the ground to wipe snow from the steps,
an hour in the shower listening to "River" on repeat,
a short, ugly haircut, it's coming out in clumps…
Oh, and when will my performance ever be enough?

Harsheni Maniarasan

LOVE AT TWENTY

A thousand stars across a black sky.
In the cold wind, we hold hands,

fingers interlaced as we walk
down a lane lined with Sacred Fig trees

dimly illuminated by street lamps.
Wandering in the gloaming

we watch our shadows,
two silhouettes moving abreast

on the pebbled path.
Our shoulders graze,

the warmth between our bodies
growing, our secret meeting

shielded by the trees
and a terrace of pastel houses.

On nights like this,
we do not need words.

Émilie Galindo

LIKE A NETTLE-NEUROTIC MOTH

You flutter petal
playful lashes / a knee jerk
bee's knees reflex / only when
the sky is bannered blackbird
beak's orange / then you feel it
creep in / the nettlesome-ness
a moth to shame / so you blow
petal-lashed wishes.

Jessie Anne Harrison

THEY JUST KEEP MOVING THE LINE

After S.M.A.S.H.

In high school my director always said
Either lose fifteen pounds or gain it
because Broadway only has room
for whisper-thin or plus-size,
and to them fifteen pounds is the difference.
I lost twenty and an agent said
Lose ten or gain five
because the camera is unforgiving,
and 90% of women in Hollywood are underweight.
I gained enough muscle that I appeared
twenty-five pounds smaller,
but I gained ten pounds in the process,
so it became *Lose five or gain ten*
and I learned to like rice cakes and pickles and arugula,
conned myself into tasting chocolate in laxatives,
and when I lost thirty pounds I got told
Sick girls can't last six shows a week in character heels
and they were right,
but I started getting cast as all the ingenues,
and the critics never speak about my acting or voice,
but all the reviews call me *beautiful*.

Maria D. Pivoda

SILENCE BETWEEN SONGS

A breath of fresh air
After spending an eternity far away, under the ocean.
For the first time in a long time,
I can hear the birds — really hear them,
singing the hymn of sunrise, telling me
To breathe out my sorrows.

I'm forever trying to name that faint,
inexplicable ache beside my heart.
Telling me to endure, to walk, to crawl
if I must.
At the end of the road, I can see something—
and right now, it seems like it will always
be just that: something.

I can hear you. I feel the warmth,
Of your memory. But it is so far away,
Who are you? How will I find you? And why must you
sing to me
in the form of birds in the trees
that line the pathway to my home.

Perhaps I was not meant to be here
Perhaps the Universe carried me away
on a different current,
lost its hold on me,
and I washed ashore here. In a sea of things and people
who can't hear my voice.

Maybe in a different lifetime.

EN ROUTE

1/ ATTACHMENT DETACHED

I thought you're the home
To my little bird as to my
Large soul
              But alas, I find
You are just another hotel
Along the long way to Dao

2/ NIGHT VISION

As the tide surges forward
From the heart of the ocean
A tiny white flower
              Is blooming
Against all the dark noises
Rising high along the coast

3/ CELEBRATION OF SUNLIGHT

Stop, Seeker, and set yourself
In a moment of meditation

If you listen to the sunshine
With all your inner & outer ears
              You would hear
A serene song of serendipities

Author's note: *Attachment Detached* was inspired by Qi
Hong (祁红).

K. Fern Lauth

BETWEEN BUILDINGS

sliver of space beckons
lures and haunts

gravitational pull
defined by absence
causing profundity
such unrelenting dignity

my monolith, my mystery

recall - A Street (1926)
(-the local heroine-)
and I fall so deep into that time

into the vacuum
feel dry and hot air
sun direct, unapologetic
absorb the soft pinks and oranges
of that sky bidding good evening
to the brown, pristine and wild landscape
that I know better than my own reflection
crumble dry, hot earth in grateful hands
inhale lightly scented sagebrush

scream of an ambulance
agitated dog bark
delivers me back
jolted
expelled with such harshness
from the veil

concrete under me
to my left
to my right
but in the atmosphere
the specter loiters

i am of this time, again

must honor, give thanks
for the parallel

Jonathan Chibuike Ukah

THE SWELTERING BEACH

Naked, I stumbled down the sweltering beach
where other nature men and women played,
children scooped up sand with wet palms
and splashed water on their watching mates.

The trees swayed; flowers waved and whispered,
above the plum tree, the bountiful fruits hung,
waiting to be plucked and rolled in their mouths
before the rapacious wind would strike them down.

I heard the harsh whistling of the misty sun
like a referee declaring open the start of games;
beckoning us to haul the ball to the middle field
where the grass pulsated, the wind assaulted.

Far from the revving crowd, the seagull hovered,
the clear skies rushed to meet the swelling sea
where the cuckoo whined; the swallows' swarm
to make hay before the looming clouds plunged in.

We slapped our backs against the sweltering beach,
where a soft breeze brushed over our sunny faces;
when we turned to glory in the heated shade
the sound of approaching rain deafening our ears.

NOTES FROM A DISRUPTOR

i've learned the acoustics of empty spaces, how a house
echoes differently when you don't plug every socket
with entertainment & every weekend isn't a marathonic
sprint of highlight reels & unnecessary consumption &
yet, when my hands & mind stay busy, i am at my best
& creating from the existence surrounding me & driving
the generational car with a screwed on bumper through
the neighborhood & not caring what people think of me
because my wealth is not measured in "things" & rather
measured in the abundance of connection with those
whom fill my life with unconditional love & continue to
show up, no matter how blistering the winds may be &
still i know there is more i can return to mother earth.

Mark Kessinger

MID

In mid morn
wife comes home
loaded with groceries
and this idea
in mid trip, mid store
in the vegetable aisle
that

on our trip traversing the gulf
west to east and back
we could forgo restaurants
for rest stop picnics,
mid way.

walk around, eat better,
save time being waited on,
save money, and, I could take
my six pictures.

I love how she reduces my
amateur mania to something
like a carnival game.
six pack of shots.
Six shooter?
How kind.

Interesting to see myself
her way, tossing out my
singular net of shuttering
six or five or seven times

at a time, when inspired,
when taken, or struck.

She says, in mid conversation,
think about it.
I say, reflexively,
OK.

CS Crowe

SNOW ON THE SAW PALM

On a winter morning in the Florida Panhandle,
Snow dusts the fronds of the saw palm, the palmetto.

A sign, Welcome to Florida, the Sunshine State,
Stays home with a warm mug of hot chocolate.
Rows of yellow pines finally understand
What it means to be an evergreen.
Snow day adult-sized children make snowmen
In sunglasses, strawhats, and bikinis.
Somewhere, an orange grove sleeps.

When the sun shines on the lustrous dust,
Nitid and gelid rime bridges the luminous and
numinous.
Is it more or less beautiful because the world is burning?

THE TIME HAS COME

The time has come to learn a
new language, to cast off the
semantics of frost, of hail-
storm and snow, ice-bound
mornings, the dark of evening,
to learn again to listen for
the voice of the swallow, the
swifts that have returned to
chorus the newly bound season,
to recall the vocabulary of
birth, hear anew the cries of
the new-born lambs that trust
in a view of pale hills, the
glimpse of eternity afforded
to them, the hollowed voice
of a moon wan in a washed-out
sky expressing itself through
the wash of waves on a shore we
will yet come to see but
struggle always to understand.

Liam Strong

RELATIVELY STABLE DECLINE

after Laurie Clements Lambeth

the stress ball conforms to its given hand. the nurse
practitioner says can you move your hands. i say yes but.
she says then you're mobile. glass wrinkles like a tissue
into a palm. the physician who smells of lysol & offers
me a muffin in the past tense. the countertop from an
airbnb i stayed in somewhere close to st louis, a sink
amputated from a garage. hotels have had better art.
sometimes my ankles can't twist or turn, i say, but other
parts of me are very flexible. i can touch all of my back
with both arms, i say, for instance. are you in pain, they
say. is discomfort pain, i say. stress poofs outward as ice
from underfoot. the affirmation, logo, phone number
peel off, live beneath my fingernails. they say no. oh, i
say. i've held planets, squeezed them against my thumb
on the back of my parents' trampoline. circles into
corkscrews. spinal springs, leverage between strength
that was never there. it's unfortunate to think that the
stress ball will too be subjugated with its own crumbling.
can i just go home, i say. my parents never held my hand
crossing the street, so it must mean i don't stay con-
nected, right. we have more paperwork to fill out, other
questions to ask, they say. i can do them myself if you'd
prefer, i suggest. the body is a resistant, tense flatline. i'm
here to make your jobs easier, not harder, i say. i know
the answers.

44

ON JARVIS CREEK

The wood stork landed in a whoosh
and a flurry, shoulders broad
as a stevedore, wrinkled bald head,
bright eyes staring. Wings white as angels
visiting in stained glass morning light.

Solemn, he started the dance, forward
three steps, half turn wing-shimmy three steps
back, beak raised then head thrust down, step
step, step, shimmy turn, furl wings.
Offshore in deep water, unblinking

the alligator watched, a dreadnought
at rest. No one else was there
to see but me on my morning
walk with the sun as the stork danced,
fluffed his ruff of down, shaking

his tail feathers, maybe in practice
for courtship. Maybe a dance of defiance,
a wing fingered gesture to all alligators.
Maybe dancing in that sheer joy
of being alive and able to fly away.

Stephen Barile

DAM 3

Smallest of the original three
Large, steel-reinforced
Concrete dams,
Across rugged and rocky
Big Creek Canyon,
To impound snowmelt
From 1913 spring-runoff.
The basin was transformed
Into *Huntington* Lake.
A camp for laborers,
Teamsters, and drillers
Near the jobsite had advantages.
Workers building Dam 3
Lived in Camp *1E*
At the west end of the basin.
Clearing and excavating started
In the summer of 1912,
Guy-derricks, and skips
Used in digging were erected.
Shrieks from locomotive whistles,
And clanging bells
Made the empty lake bottom
Like a main-line railyard.
Thunder from dynamite explosions
Echoed, and reverberated
From the canyon walls
Up and down, across and back.
The early days of the project,
Drilling was done by hand,
Single and double-jack.

A drill in one hand,
Sledge-hammer in the other.
Work commenced in spring,
Crews were busy, since building
The dams had stopped
Over winter's heavy snowfall.
Excavation began downstream,
A new section was poured.
Pneumatic drills pounded away
Boring holes for steel-rails
From abandoned portions
Of the lake-bottom railroad.
Reinforcement to hold
The new concrete to the old.
Carpenters and laborers, like ants
Busy building forms and chutes
To convey wet concrete.
When the dam was near completion
Workmen moved on to Dam #2.

Ananthan K P

BEREFT

Aadila, where are you?
you've left me no trace to reach you
each way I proceed, yet
am stuck, hindered
from moving any further
in a hundred ways I try to reach you
and fail miserably
you've seen to it so carefully
for me
that all ways leading to you are shut.
bereft of your help, a multitude
of ways claim me
all dull, descending,
leading none nowhere
bereft of a helping hand, see
an abandoned wretch I roam
in the routeless desert
yet abounding with love
for you
yearning

Aadila,
I'm the bunny rabbit lost in a labyrinth
who'll show me the way to reach home?

Ephraim Scott Sommers

ODE TO ALL THE FAILED POEMS TOO

My heart pills and vitamins and insulin pens
        and monitor kits and boxes of glucagon

and extra sensors and glucose tablets in a Ziploc bag
        in my grey lunch box,

        I have the almonds and celery and tuna cans
enough
to make it across a whole continent. I have other
people's poems,

humanity's great ledger of emotional pursuits,
        open in my lap,
and nothing today to make of my own.
        The purpose of this trip has always been
        to land in a better life,
and I could almost be a train station
        in Kalamazoo,
the way some days like this seem to appear here
        and empty themselves

and refill themselves and then quickly depart.
Gone to Chicago or Omaha to be something more for
somebody else.

        Arriving on time in a different body is impossible

now. Some days, like a failed novel, don't change me at
the end
into a vial full

Ode to All the Failed Poems Too

of my own escaping. I must dwell instead in what
I'm incapable of

while the words pass through me like passengers
I don't notice. Like failed symbols representative of
nothing

but themselves, like a melody (at the edge of this
moment)
that just doesn't matter

as much as anyone searching through their belongings
for their camera
wants it to. I always want epiphany to arrive

at the end
of turbulence.

All I am, today, though, is the space that is left
when it doesn't.

All I am, today, is a plane, parked for the
evening,
left empty
in the dark, after so much bumping into clouds,

hoping for a much better pilot
and crew and path and fuel and flight
manifest tomorrow,

as if the record of what we take inside of us and what
we have let go of

and how we don't get where we want

is as important as getting there at all. I do want to
remember this
throb, though, my ears squeaking fully open
                            as the pressure equalizes

between where I've been and what I wanted and where
I am,
at closing time, someone in a work-boots following a
buffing machine across a gunked floor.

This hum here is all mine.
This memorial is for one more day I failed

at making a medicine capable of changing my life,
and so tumbled more unapologetically into this new
place,

this place where all the dead chess pieces and ghost
unicorns have gathered beside me,
this place that looks almost like acceptance.

Gabriel Noel

THE DIALECT OF WEEPING WILLOWS

As soon
as the earth starts to warm
you trod barefoot to the willows.

Through the panes of glass
I watch you write love notes
on the backs of their branches.

I watch you sharpen your pencil
                    blade
into a fine point,
sharp enough to draw sap
                    blood
out of the trees you so tenderly grasp.
You pray the birds learn the
melody to your last ditch swan song.

You forget
that willows speak through the breeze
that passes between leaves
just as we speak through breaths
passed between mouthfuls
of each other.

        Tongue
                to bark
to   sap
back to   tongue.

I am fluent in your mouth
and you are fluent in mine.

Steve Denehan

DRIVING HOME FROM CARLOW

Empty roads through quilted farms
morning heat and summer music
Friesians stand in uniform
black and white on green

the gleaming rapeseed fields
hillside peels of fallen sunshine
even all of this
is not enough

Starry Krueger

REASONS TO KEEP GOING

Andi
Sent a crystal necklace
And a card with a bike,
"Keep going."

Sam
Left work early
Bought flowers and pizza
bites
So aggressively delicious
The sauce burned my leg.

Danny
Greeted me with a pirate
accent.

Ricardo
Handed me half of his burrito.

Julie
Got lost with me
Exploring the water's edge
Chasing phantom
Sea creatures
In the dark.

Brian
Walked out of the waves
Seaweed tangled in his long
hair

And lead me to a secret garden.
Played the violin
Cooked me salmon

Last week in a coffee shop
You asked,
"With so much pain in the
world,
Why do we keep going?"

For angels and pizza bites
For pirates and burritos
For eyes that translate
hearts
For the mystery
For momentum
For each other

For the miracle
That your kindness
Might save
A life.

TO IRIS ABOUT HERSELF

Icon of summer, Iris,
mere-maid, artiste youth
in her crayon's color intense
childhood's paradise

Purple is the New Black
Midnight Blue in light
summer night of fireflies
like Electric Lime

Kitty Kat Black
Shadow of a dream below
cartwheeling kite
ferris wheel

glows in Cosmic Black
Midnight rainbow carnival
kaleidoscope
carousel lit

Neon, in Carrot Orange,
Jazzberry Jam
whirligig Sunflower on Desert Sand,
Purple Mountains Majesty,

Magic Potion scents of cotton candy
Pixie Dust yellow wiles away awhile
White Confetti Glitter stars
sparkling forever and a day

where silverware left

To Iris About Herself

out in slender rain
swing sets, jungle gym
seesaws

your wavelength of good vibes,
ice cream freeze
Pearly White curl
on the picnic beach

Surfs Up, Pacific Blue
awhile ago whimsical squeeze
a childlike crystal memory disappears
In salty tears

Inchworm, Light Green
Lizard tan
On their tiny grave, gone home
Tidily I've set this stone.

————

If I were the queen Bee

I'd entitle you, golden One of the bumblebees
if there were still wild hedges of bramble berries
in glowing haze, or a lazy motion in a swarm
to dream of, keep me warm, summertime morn.

Both alive a day to mourn, Saint John's day lovers'
the flowers frail fairy pollen, midsummer's
drowsy fantasy of famous charm, being your
fate as if royal days of yore.

It was a day, of mythical import,
a year and one day for a queen's consort

to live, to dream, to give all wisdom mirth
cross-pollinated good earth.

MF Charles

HIS RUDDY FACE TENDED TO THE FIELDS

in a sun bleached shirt, small offset buttonhole in the
pocket for a pencil, gauging the chance of rains. Brief
gusts triggered waves of susurrations among the dry
corn husks. He sat on the chipped concrete side of the
empty cistern. Its edge cast a small smidgeon of shade
for a barrel of a dog laid belly-down, head on its paws
ears drooping, an occasional chuff stirring up pale dust.
At the stream, a tree listened to the shlooping sound
of cow hooves ambling along through the last of the
mud, searching for a slurp of water their socks of lead-
en colored mud flaked and dried. Faraway, an unheard
vibration, whipping west wind & towering iron cumulus
clouds laid the first drops of rain raising small puffs in
the dry dust . Released in drenching waves, flowed down
his face. Some of it was salty.

BIOGRAPHIES

Carter Vance is a writer and poet originally from Cobourg, Ontario, Canada currently resident in Gatineau, Quebec, Canada. His work has appeared in such publications as *The Smart Set*, *Contemporary Verse 2* and *A Midwestern Review*, amongst others. His debut novel, *Smaller Animals*, will be published in Fall 2025.

DS Maolalai has been described by one editor as "a cosmopolitan poet" and another as "prolific, bordering on incontinent." His work has nominated thirteen times for Best of the Net, ten for the Pushcart and once for the Forward Prize, and has been released in three collections: *Love is Breaking Plates in the Garden* (Encircle Press, 2016), *Sad Havoc Among the Birds* (Turas Press, 2019) and *Noble Rot* (Turas Press, 2022).

Gabrielle DeWeese is a writer who grew up in the verdant Southeast but now calls the desert of Tucson, Arizona home. She loves to read literature in translation and doodle in her sketchbook. Her short fiction can be found in *Pine Reads Review*. This is her first time being featured in a publication for her poetry.

Cecil Morris, a retired teacher, has poems appearing in *2River View*, *Common Ground Review*, *Hole in the Head Review*, *Lascaux Review*, *Rust + Moth*, and elsewhere. His debut poetry collection, *At Work in the Garden of Possibilities*, will come out from Main Street Rag in 2025. He and his wife, mother of their children, divide their year between the relatively hot Central Valley of California and the cool Oregon coast.

Kenneth Kesner (肯内思) splits his time between the Caucasus and South East Asia. Some recent works are featured in: *Choeofplerin Press, the engine(idling, Flora Fiction, Pictura Journal,* and *Plato's Caves.*

Kora Dzbinski (he/they) is a Mad-queer poet and scholar based in Chicago, where they write about Madness, transness, disability, horror, film, and sex work. They hope you are drinking enough water. Find them on everything as @oatmilkmom.

Leda Muscatello (she/her) resides in the foothills of the Blue Ridge Mountains of Virginia. Her inspirations include table wine, thrift store art, and antique keys. Leda was forged in a culture of mountain lore with a family that made music and told stories because it was carved into the surface of their bones. She has been married to her partner (an artist and poet) for almost 18 years, has 4 children and 1 bonus child, and works as a Domestic Violence Advocate. Her work can be found, most recently, in *Sequoia Speaks* and *New Feathers Anthology.*

Dorit d'Scarlett is a Danish-Australian writer unexpectedly living in the tropics. Her short stories and prize-winning poetry have featured in international literary journals, and her long-form fiction has been short-listed for multiple writing awards. As a minority immigrant at school, she faced cultural bullying, and those challenges deeply inform her work, shaping exploration of identity, belonging, and the emotional landscapes of those caught between worlds. She can usually be found with too many tabs open, a martini as dry as her hope for humanity, or on Insta as @dorit_dscarlett_writer

Hugh Findlay's writing and photography has been published worldwide. Nominated for a Pushcart Prize in 2020 for poetry, and the Best Microfiction Anthology 2024, he is in the third trimester of life and hopes y'all like his stuff. Instagram: @hughmanfindlay

An award-winning writer and artist, **Karen Pierce Gonzalez**'s chapbooks include *Coyote in the Basket of My Ribs* (Kelsay Books), *Moon kissed Earth wrought Vision drunk* (Bottlecap Press), *Down River with Li Po* (Black Cat Poetry Press), *Sun and Moon Wired Together* (Midsummer Dream House), *Mountains of Ocean:10 Waves and RavenSong* (Poetic Librettos/Four Feathers Press). To date 75+ of her intuitive artworks have been published in a range of chapbooks and journals, including Hedgehog Poetry Press's Little Black Book (with Marcelle Newbold), and *Chestnut Review*. And she does all this in the verdant rural landscape of San Francisco's North Bay.

Maggie Fulmer (she/her) lives in Northern Kentucky, works in Cincinnati, Ohio and writes wherever she can. She is a founding editor of the indie literary magazine *Many Nice Donkeys*. You can find her on most corners of the internet (@mfulms21) talking about boy bands, books, and her AMC A-List subscription. She can not do a cartwheel.

Zach Spruce (he/him) is the author of the chapbook *Vanishing Sun from Bottlecap Press* (2024). Zach holds a bachelor's degree in creative writing and film studies from SUNY Brockport. His work has been featured or is forthcoming in *Wild Roof Journal, The Closed Eye Open, Serotonin Press, Lucky Jefferson, Bare Hill Review*, and *Lilac Mag*. He is currently pursuing a master's degree in social work and has worked as a crisis counselor for 988 Lifeline. He lives in Upstate New York and enjoys specialty coffee, Polaroids, and getting lost in the woods. Find him on

Instagram @mkultramagickcult

James Broschart is a child of the Depression and grew up in small-town Pennsylvania. He is retired from careers in classroom teaching, public television production, technical writing, and bookstore management. He has written about lifelong learning, safe schools, and marine science for various federal agencies. He taught English composition to sailors at sea and developed emergency management manuals for U.S. nuclear sites. Having lived through the terms of fifteen U.S. presidents he is eager to see what will happen next.

Naudia Reeves is a queer poet with an MFA in Creative Writing. Born and raised in Florida and now living in Michigan, her work dwells in themes of queerness, grief, intimacy, and self-interrogation. She writes with a quiet lyricism, often drawing from memory, landscape, and the rhythms of everyday life—with the occasional interruption from one of her four unruly cats, or five darling rats. Her poems have appeared in *The Passionfruit Review, Progenitor, LETTERS Journal,* and elsewhere.

Taylor Necko has BFA in Creative Writing from Bowling Green State University, where she served as Editor in Chief of *Prairie Margins* and wrote for Her Campus BGSU. Much of her creative work is focused on human relationships and how they transform. She has been published in *Gabby and Min's Literary Review, Route 7 Review, Periphery Journal, The Ear,* and *Oakland Arts Review.*

Yvonne Higgins Leach is the author of a poetry collection *In the Spaces Between Us* (Kelsay Books 2024). Her first collection *Another Autumn* was published by Cherry Grove Collections in 2014. She spent decades balancing a career in communications and public relations, raising a family, and pursuing her love of writing poetry. Her latest passion is working with shelter dogs. She splits her time living on Vashon Island and in Spokane, Washington.

Kirby Michael Wright was a guest lecturer at Trinity College Dublin. He lives beside the track in Del Mar with his wife Darcy and a cat named Gatsby.

Michael Theroux writes from his home in Northern California. His career has spanned field botanist, environmental health specialist, green energy developer and resource recovery web site editor. Now, to exercise the other side of his brain: entering the field in his seventh decade, Michael is now seeking publication of his cache of creative, literary writings. Many may be found in *Ariel Chart*, *50WS*, *CafeLit*, *Poetry Pacific*, *Last Leaves*, *Backwards Trajectory*, *Small Wonders*, *Cerasus*, *Acedian Review*, the *Lothlorien Poetry*, *City Key*, *Wild Word*, *Fixator Press* and elsewhere.

Ruth Ticktin resides in Chesapeake Beach, Maryland. Writing poetry, prose, dreams and discoveries, Ruth encourages sharing stories. She is a teacher and an author: *Around & Around Poetry Chapbook* (BottlecapPress 2024;) *Was, Am, Going, Recollections in Poetry & Flash* (New Bay Books, 2022;) *What's Ahead?* (Pro Lingua Learning 2013, coauthor.) a contributor: *Press Pause Press* #6, 4/22; *Bright Flash* 9/24; *Dulcet Lit* 11/24 and more.

Amelia Napiorkowski lives outside of Washington, DC on the Chesapeake Bay with her husband, son, and step-daughters. In 2025, she quit her government job in intelligence to stay at home with her baby and pursue her passion for creative writing. Her work has appeared in *wildscape. literary journal*, the *Broken Teacup*, and *Mania Magazine*.

Harsheni Maniarasan is a MA Creative Writing student at University of Bristol who possesses a huge affinity for literature and spends most of her time reading and penning poetry. She holds a particular interest in ghazals, haikus and exploring nature through imagery and narratives. She also loves puppies, singing and learning new languages - she knows six as of now! Presently, she works as a Poetry Editor at *The Poetry Lighthouse*.

Jake Williams is a writer and photographer based in Cumbria. He was born in deepest rural Dorset the year Marvin Gaye asked what's going on, in a cottage with Owls in the attic and a serious damp problem. Basically, he was Feral Kid from Mad Max 2 if he'd been a character in a Thomas Hardy novel. The woods and fields were as much his classroom as any of the schools he attended. As well as ranging across the countryside, he enjoys ranging widely across disciplines and following his creativity down paths less travelled. Not to mention eating Tofu.

Growing up, **Émilie Galindo** felt that subtext & symbols loomed over her childhood. As she watched her family trip over their own patterns, she couldn't help but become wary of what she loved most: storytelling (and its pretty patterns). That's why her writing aims to question the myriads of surrealistic motifs, motives & mementos stowed away in our anecdotes or homespun narratives. Also, her debut novella *Acid Taste: Excavating the Homesick's Blues* is out thanks to the wonderful support of Querencia press.

Jessie Anne Harrison (she/her) has had a fascination with poetry since she was nine. As she pursues an MFA in Creative Writing from Arcadia University, she explores themes of faith, identity reconstruction, and grief. Her work is previously featured in *The Prose*, *2River View*, and *Mobius: Journal for Social Change*.

Maria D. Pivoda is a multidisciplinary artist working in both digital and traditional media. Originally from Romania, she is currently studying at South Gate Creative Writing School in Denmark. Her work explores the human condition and the power of the mind. In 2023, she completed her first novel, *Whisper of The Wind*, and is currently working on its sequel, *City of Cyne*. Since 2018, Maria has specialized in commissioned character design and portraiture.

Yuan Changming grew up in an isolated village, started to learn the English alphabet in Shanghai at age nineteen and published monographs on translation before leaving China. With a Canadian PhD in English, Yuan currently lives in Vancouver, where he co-edits *Poetry Pacific* with Allen Yuan. His writing credits include 16 solo chapbooks, 12 Pushcart nominations for poetry and 3 for fiction besides appearances in The Best of the Best Canadian Poetry (2008-17), BestNewPoemsOnline and 2149 other publications across 51 countries. A poetry judge for Canada's 44th National Magazine Awards, Yuan began writing and publishing fiction in 2022. His debut novel *Detaching*, 'silver romance' *The Tuner* and short story collection *Flashbacks* are all available at Amazon.

K. Fern Lauth is a writer who enjoys exploring the expansive nature of the conscious and the subconscious, the peculiar boundary of those states, the truth that discovery reveals and how it unites us all. When not self-indulgently writing free verse poetry, she spends her time attempting to be a redeemable human and with her beloved muse, her Zebra.

Jonathan Chibuike Ukah is a Pushcart-nominated poet living in the United Kingdom. His poems have been featured in, TABs The Journal of Arts and Poetics, After Happy Hour Magazine, The Pierian, Propel Magazine, the Island of Wak-Wak, The Journal of Undiscovered Poets and elsewhere. He won the Poet of the Month at the Literary Shark Magazine for February 2025. He was Finalist at the Four Tulips Poetry Contest 2025 and the Third Prize Winner at the Anansi Archive Poetry Contest 2025. He was the Third Prize Winner at The Hemlock Journal Poetry Contest 2025. Facebook/ Instagram: Chibuikeukasoanya. Twitter: Johnking1502

Eileen Porzuczek is a creative writer and professional storyteller in Greater Indianapolis. She is the author of the poetry collection *Memento Mori: A Poetic Memoir in Three Parts* (Finishing Line Press, 2025). Eileen's poems also appear in *So It Goes: The Journal of the Kurt Vonnegut Museum and Library, Creation Magazine, New Plains Review, Tulsa Review,* and more. In her free time, she enjoys playing cards and eating spicy food.

Mark Kessinger was born in Huntington WV, attended college at Cleveland State University, lived in Oklahoma City and now resides in Houston TX. He is a two-year recipient of a creative writing scholarship from CSU, a founding member and former president of the Houston Council of Writers, and former editor of *Voices from Big Thicket.* His poetry has appeared in many publications and four anthologies.

CS Crowe is a poet and storyteller from the Southeastern United States, he believes stories and poems are about the journey, not the destination, and he loves those stories that wander in the wilderness for forty years before finding their way to the promised land.

J.M. Summers was born and still lives in South Wales. Previous publication credits include *Another Country* from Gomer Press and various magazines / anthologies. The former editor of a number of small press magazines, he is currently working on his first collection.

Liam Strong (they/them) is a disembodied genderless question mark and the author of three chapbooks. They died in 2020 and have been writing ever since. Find them on Instagram: @beanbie666.

Poet, author and photographer, **K.L. Johnston**'s works are available in literary anthologies, magazines and journals. Best known for regional works and poetry centered in spiritual experience, nature, and trauma survival, she has released two collections of poetry into the wild: *Grace Period* and *The Nature of These Gifts.* Currently retired from a stint as an antiques and art dealer, she lives and works near the banks of the Savannah River.

Stephen Barile, an award-winning poet and 2023 Pushcart Prize nominee, is a Fresno, California native. He attended Fresno City College, Fresno Pacific University, and California State University, Fresno. He taught writing at Madera College, and CSU Fresno. His poems have been anthologized and widely published in on-line and print journals, including: *The Broad River Review,*

Featured Poets, The Heartland Review, Hellbender Magazine, Ignatian, London Grip, Mason Street Review, Midsummer Dream House, New World Writing Quarterly, The North Dakota Quarterly, The Opiate, Pharos, Rio Grande Review, Sandy River Review, San Joaquin Review, Santa Clara Review, The Scop, The Selkie, Willawaw Journal.

Born in 1992, **Ananthan K P** is an emerging poet and academic from India. He has published a number of essays in various journals globally and is currently working as a Guest Faculty in the Dept. of English at Sree Sankaracharya University of Sanskrit, Kalady, RC Panmana, Kerala.

Ephraim Scott Sommers is a Type-1 Diabetic and the author of two books: *Someone You Love Is Still Alive* (2019) and *The Night We Set the Dead Kid on Fire* (2017). Currently, he lives in Rock Hill, South Carolina and is an Associate Professor of English at Winthrop University. He is also an actively touring singer-songwriter.

Gabriel Noel (he/they) is a Pushcart Prize nominated poet who received his Bachelor's for Theatre Arts and English at Salem State University. His poetry covers themes such as human connection, grief, queer love, and nostalgia. Gabriel lives on the occupied land of Naumkeag ("fishing place") colloquially known as Salem, Massachusetts and likes to spend time with his partner

Steve Denehan lives in Kildare, Ireland with his wife Eimear and daughter Robin. He is the award-winning author of two chapbooks and seven poetry collections. and friends at concerts or karaoke.

Starry Krueger is a San Diego based writer, teacher

and director. She is the founder of Imaginary Theater Company, a theater company committed to producing original plays that empower children to be the heroes of their own stories. Her plays *Dream Train, Mama Threw Me So High, He Who Speaks* and *Canary Cockroach Phoenix* have been published by Drama Notebook. Starry is a proud member of the Dramatist's Guild and TYA/USA. (Instagram: @imaginarytheaterco)

Carolyn Mack lives in the desert mountains of San Diego with husband and pooch.

MF Charles (he/him), lives in Waverly, Iowa. Retired from academia, he reads/writes poetry, gardens, and helps others via community service. His lyric mainstream poetry is flavored by nature personified, introspection, and life's highs and lows. He writes poems to tell stories. He found that poetry's myriad ways to combine words and cadences to express ideas and emotions was the seductively creative leap that he was seeking. For him, a poem provides a chance to produce an affect — hot or cold — in his reader. He has been published in 12 literary journals including *Talon Review, The River,* and *The Stray Branch.*

Dan Ross is a community pediatrician working with kids with neurodiverse needs and profiles. In his spare time, he explores his creative side through unique images and perspectives in photography. He hopes his images touch others and evoke meaningful feelings. Instagram @eclecticimagesyyc

www.ingramcontent.com/pod-product-compliance
Lightning Source LLC
LaVergne TN
LVHW021620080426
835510LV00019B/2672